Life: Enjoy The Ride

To Baby Amon, wishing you a long and happy life, filled with Adventure. Enjoy Each Day. Enjoy The Ride!

Lee Nordy

Life: Enjoy The Ride

Lee Monday, Ph.D.

Aventine Press

© Copyright 2006 by Lee Monday, Ph.D.

First edition

Without limiting the rights under copyright reserved above, no part of this publication may be reproduced, stored in or introduced into a retrieval system, or transmitted, in any form or by any means (electronic, mechanical, photocopying, recording, or otherwise), without the prior written permission of both the copyright owner and the publisher of this book.

Aventine Press
1023 4th Avenue, Suite 204
San Diego, CA 92101

ISBN: 1-59330-348-3

Printed in the United States of America

ALL RIGHTS RESERVED

INTRODUCTION

As a psychologist in private practice, many times when patients felt "stuck" in their lives, I would tell them the story of the turtle. This simple yet powerful story illustrates why there is unhappiness in our lives and offers ways to find peacefulness.

The book uses an analogy for life - a river. We are all given a different starting point, some better than others. We have choices to make as we navigate through our lives. We are only able to see where we are now and maybe what is just ahead of us.

A river has a current that guides us and provides a more direct path. Some will consider this current a higher power, God, the force, source, energy, or nature. When we are calm, aware and focused on the present, we flow with the river and experience a full life.

Our struggles come about when we override the natural flow and allow our fear of the future or fantasies of what we want to dominate our lives. When fear is prominent our thoughts revolve around "what if" something happens in the future. Instead of enjoying and experiencing our lives, we become anxious and self limiting. In this story the turtle holds on to a rock or a branch. In life it may be a relationship, a routine, or a job.

When fantasy dominates, we go against the flow in life. Others tell us a decision is wrong or unfounded. Our instincts give us the same message, yet we go against what we know is right and follow an irrational fantasy. This often happens in relationships, where all information says that this person is not right for us, yet we want to believe that it could work. It may be the belief that a person will change. The fantasy may be of a career that you do not have the talents or personality for. Fantasy is being loosely defined as letting what we want life to be to over ride reality.

The lesson of this book is to live life in the present. To be aware enough to feel the current. To experience every moment with appreciation and awe. To deal with the future when it becomes the present. To let go of the past. To be led by what we know to be true instead of irrational fantasies. To learn that life is a journey and to enjoy the ride.

My hope is that this book is not read once and put away on a shelf. Instead let it be a visible reminder to enjoy the ride.

Life: Enjoy The Ride

Lee Monday, Ph.D.

There once was a turtle……
He was floating down a river.
He was happy and relaxed with no worries.

Life: Enjoy The Ride

Suddenly, he could feel the water moving quickly.
He saw trees, rocks and land all passing by in a blur.
Just ahead he saw a tree branch hanging over the water.
He reached out, and was able to hold on.
Holding to a nearby branch was another turtle.

"That was fun," said turtle.

The other turtle replied, "are you nuts? You could have gotten hurt. The river is dangerous, it could be even worse up ahead. It is smarter and safer to stay here."

"How long have you been here," asked turtle?

"Most of my life, this is where I live," answered the second turtle.

Life: Enjoy The Ride

*"What about exploring the river, and going as far as you can,"
asked turtle?*

"I am staying here. No one who has gone on has ever come back. I hear that there are scary things around the bend"

*Turtle asked, "don't you get tired of holding on to the branch?"
The other turtle replied, "yes, but life is difficult and tiring.
That is what life is."*

The current kept pulling on his body, urging him to go down river, yet he wondered, what if his new friend was right and there was disaster around the next bend?

The turtle heard two voices within him. There was a logical thinking part of him that knew he could trust the current, it would lead him where he needed to go. There was also a part of him that was fearful of the unknown and the possible future.

Life: Enjoy The Ride

Turtle chose to trust the current. He waved goodbye to his new friend and felt the rush of the water carrying him along.

He felt both peace and excitement as he was guided along on his journey. He was not concerned with what lies ahead. He simply enjoyed the moment.

Life: Enjoy The Ride

The water was not always smooth, yet the current always carried him through. One day when the water was a little rough, turtle saw a spot that looked good to him. It was a large flat rock in the sun, but it was not in concert with the current. Turtle could see other turtles sunning themselves on the rock. He decided that the rock was where he wanted to be. Turtle fought the current and worked his way to the rock.

Life: Enjoy The Ride

Once there he was very tired. He was about to fall asleep when he saw the shadow of a large bird, heading for him! Turtle pulled into his shell just as he felt the impact of the bird. He heard the bird pecking at him and felt the vibration. "Oh why did this happen?" "I should never have come here" Finally the pecking stopped and turtle came out of his shell. He talked to the other turtles. They had also chosen to come to the rock. They lived with the regular attacks of the birds.
This was their life.

Life: Enjoy The Ride

Turtle talked about the current of the river. How it energized him. How it led anyone who would trust it along their own individual journey. It enabled him to experience life fully. Some turtles laughed at him. Some said there was no current. Some said they were afraid to trust.

Life: Enjoy The Ride

Turtle knew that he could not stay with these turtles, this was not his place or his people. There was more life to experience. Turtle left the rock, but now had to find the current again. The river had, as it always does, changed since he had come to the rock. Turtle found that he could move with the river, yet the true current might take some effort to find.

Life: Enjoy The Ride

Lee Monday, Ph.D.

Turtle came to a fork in the river. He saw many turtles going left and a few went right. He felt the pull to the right, his instinct said right, yet he wanted to go where there seemed to be more turtles.
He trusted what he wanted over what he knew to be right for him.

Life: Enjoy The Ride

The path to the left was difficult, it was shallow and muddy for awhile. It was drudgery to walk through the mud. As you know turtles do not walk very fast. Then the water smelled awful. The slow moving water led them along with very little to see.

Turtle talked to another turtle near by. "I should have trusted the voice inside of me and gone right at that fork back there," he said.

The other turtle explained that this path looped around and they would again come to the fork. He and many others always chose the left fork.

"But why?" asked turtle.

The other explained that even though this choice always led to the mud and bad smelling water, he knew how long the mud lasted. He knew how long he would be in the bad water. He had always gone this way. There was comfort in the known, even if it was not great.

Life: Enjoy The Ride

Turtle talked about trusting the current. It would carry them to new and exciting places.

No, this other turtle and surprisingly many others chose to take the known path and repeat the pattern.

When the fork came up this time, turtle was sure to take the right fork. It was not long before he was again carried by the current.

Life: Enjoy The Ride

He passed other turtles holding on to sticks and more turtles glued to rocks, afraid and tired.

Life: Enjoy The Ride

Turtle saw whirlpools on the side of the river that went round and round.
Some chose to stay in this never ending circle.
He saw many fighting the current.

Life: Enjoy The Ride

He felt that he was a part of the river. He was at peace.

Life: Enjoy The Ride

It wasn't long before the river suddenly pulled him under water. He panicked and started thrashing. Was he going to drown? He couldn't find his way to the surface.

A voice in his head said, "relax, trust the river, don't fight it." On one level he was afraid to drown and on another level he knew the current always led him to where he needed to be.

Turtle closed his eyes, relaxed and felt the current carry him… to the surface. He took a deep breath.

Life: Enjoy The Ride

Turtle experienced a wonderful life. He saw as much of the river as he could. The current took him along his path. Turtle did not worry about the future, the current would help him find his way if difficult times arose. Turtle did not dwell on the past, it was behind him now.

Life: Enjoy The Ride

Turtle shared his belief about the current with others, hoping to help them find their path in life. He understood that we all begin in different places on the river, some having an easier start than others.

Life: Enjoy The Ride

We often fight against the current. Sometimes because of fear. Sometimes because of a fantasy of the way we want life to be. Sometimes because we find comfort in repeating patterns.

There is a voice that guides us. We have to learn to hear it and trust it. To flow with the river. To enjoy the ride.

Life: Enjoy The Ride

THE END

DISCUSSION QUESTIONS

What does the metaphor of the river mean in the story?

Give an example of a time in your life when you went against the current and this created difficulty for you.

How did you know you were going against the current? How did you feel?

Why did you go against the current?

How has fear of the future been a factor in your life? How did this fear affect your life?

Describe a time where you were led by your wanting a person or situation to be different then they were.

Where in your life have you been stuck in a whirlpool? How did you get out?

Is this story implying that fantasy is a negative thing?

In the book the author uses the term "repeating patterns." What does he mean by this and have you done this in your life?

Describe a time when you were in concert with the river and perfectly at peace.

Life: Enjoy The Ride

Notes

Notes

Printed in the United States
45037LVS00001B/1063-1569